Calvin Tibbets: Oregon's First Pioneer

ALLEN DAVY
JOSEPH HOLMAN
JOHN EDMUNDS
JOSEPH GALE
RUSSELL OSBORN
DAVID WESTON
WILLIAM JOHNSON
W. HAUXHURST
WILLIAM CANNON
MEDOREM CRAWFORD
JOHN L. MORRISON
P. M. ARMSTRONG
CALVIN TIBBETTS
J. R. ROBB
SOLOMON H. SMITH
A. E. WILSON
F. X. MATTHIEU
ETIENNE LUCIER

ERECTED ON
THURSDAY MAY 2,1901
IN HONOR OF THE
FIRST AMERICAN
GOVERNMENT
ON THE PACIFIC COAST
ORGANIZED HERE
TUESDAY MAY 2,1843
52 PERSONS VOTING
FOR, 50 AGAINST,
THE NAMES OF THE FORMER
AS FAR AS OBTAINABLE
ARE HEREON
INSCRIBED.

Monument in the Champoeg State Historic Area where a vote on May 2, 1843 established "the first American government on the Pacific Coast." Calvin Tibbetts [*Tibbets*] is listed among those voting in favor. Photo by author.

Calvin Tibbets: Oregon's First Pioneer

Jerry Sutherland

Calvin Tibbets: Oregon's First Pioneer was first published as a two-part article in the Fall 2014 and Winter 2015 issues of *Cumtux*, the Clatsop County Historical Society quarterly journal. Several images have been added, a few dropped, and most captions changed. Text and citations have been edited and updated as needed.

Front Cover: Drawing of a fur trapper, page 145 of *In wilden Westen, eine Künstlerfahrt durch die Prairien und Felsengebirge der Union*, by Rudolf Cronau (1890). No image of Calvin Tibbets has been found.

Dedicated to my father, Art Sutherland, whose inexorable interest in Calvin Tibbets ultimately inspired my own. This book would not have been written without him.

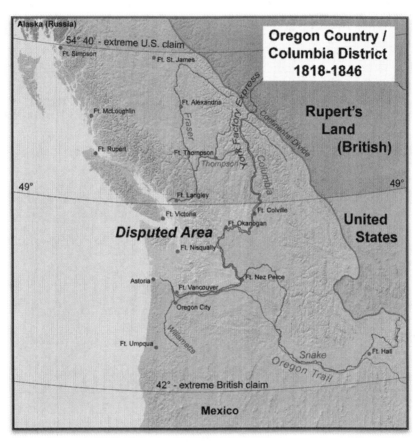

Map showing the most extreme claims of the United States (Oregon Country) and Great Britain (Columbia District) from 1818 to 1846.[3]

At noon on October 29, 1832, eleven American men and their leader, Nathaniel Wyeth, arrived at Fort Vancouver, operations hub for the Hudson's Bay Company (HBC) in Oregon Country.[1] Chief Factor John McLoughlin greeted them cordially, despite knowing that Wyeth was there to compete with him and suspecting that he was affiliated with Hall Kelley, who planned to build a colony in Oregon as the first step in making it part of the United States.[2] Eventually, both Wyeth and Kelley would fail in their ventures, but one of the men they brought to Oregon—Calvin Tibbets—stayed to make it his home and pave the way for other Americans to follow. In doing so, this obscure fellow would become Oregon's first pioneer without anyone—including himself—recognizing it.

Oregon statehood may seem inevitable today, but in 1832 it was not. The United States and Great Britain had agreed to joint occupation of Oregon Country as an expedient way to end the War of 1812, but in the meantime the HBC had built a commercial empire that no American enterprise had been able to compete with. The monopoly charter and powers of state granted the HBC by Great Britain gave it virtual control of Oregon Country.[3] A few years before Wyeth's group arrived, HBC retirees had started settling along the Willamette River. Since the British negotiators had told their American counterparts that the "rights of exclusive sovereignty . . . would someday come to the nation that settled the country," Oregon was looking more British than American.[4]

The American pioneers who flooded into Oregon in the 1840s eventually turned the tide, but timing, politics, and other factors came into play. A few members of Congress began pushing for American acquisition of Oregon Country soon after the War of 1812 ended, but they met resistance, especially from Southern Democrats who wanted nothing to do with adding new territory populated with non-whites. As disease brought by whites killed off Oregon's Indians, the racial mix became more acceptable to them.[5] Some of the American pioneers threatened the HBC with violence, damage, and theft—to the extent that McLoughlin's supervisor, Governor George Simpson, moved the Columbia District headquarters to Fort Victoria on Vancouver Island in 1845 just to get away from them.[6] By then the HBC had trapped out most of the beaver population in Oregon Country and the European market for beaver hats was declining, so the HBC had little to lose. And though they had increased in number, British citizens in Oregon were just too few to justify war. This left British negotiators at a disadvantage with their American counterparts. If the HBC no longer cared that much about Oregon, how could they pretend a willingness to fight for it?[7]

In contrast, American negotiators were being instructed to play hardball by James Polk, an expansionist president whose Democratic Party had started a campaign with the slogan "Fifty-Four Forty or Fight." A growing number of American citizens living in Oregon—who had petitioned the United States to acquire them, and had taken the initiative to form an independent government when they were ignored—gave Polk the kind of leverage he needed to carry out his agenda with the British and his own Congress. The Oregon Treaty of 1846 gave all of the Oregon Country south of the forty-ninth parallel, except for Vancouver Island and some of its surrounding islands, to the United States.[8]

Given the critical role they played in making Oregon part of the United States, it is surprising that no American has previously been identified as Oregon's first pioneer.[9] Ironically, the British claimed one of their own for the distinction. A 1908 book review of *Dr. John McLoughlin, the*

Father of Oregon in the Royal Geographic Society's *The Geographic Journal* said, "This is a simple and interesting record of the career of the first pioneer of Oregon."[10] The book's author, Frederick Holman, was President of the Oregon Historical Society (OHS). He clearly intended giving tribute to McLoughlin for assisting so many Americans when they first arrived in Oregon, but he did not refer to him as an Oregon pioneer. Those pioneers still alive then who had received McLoughlin's aid would most likely have agreed with Holman in calling him the "Father of Oregon," but they never would have considered him one of their own, much less first. [11] They had trudged two thousand miles to claim free land in Oregon for themselves. To achieve that, Oregon would have to become part of the United States, and for that to happen they would have to push McLoughlin's HBC out of the way.[12]

Photo of John McLoughlin, opposite page 104 of *The Centennial History of Oregon, 1811-1912, Volume 1*, by Joseph Gaston (1912).

The Royal Geographic Society was obviously taking liberties with the definition of "pioneer" in reference to Oregon. When used for other purposes, or even applied to other American states, that might be acceptable. However, the phrase "Oregon pioneer" has a well-established connotation (wagon trains crossing the Oregon Trail) that needs to be taken into account by the criteria used for identifying Oregon's first pioneer: he or she must have been the first American to come to Oregon with the intent to settle permanently and make it part of the United States. The first white men to visit Oregon do not qualify because they were explorers, scientists, soldiers, fur trappers (including John McLoughlin and other HBC employees), sailors, and entrepreneurs, not colonizers.[13]

It is important to recognize that Oregon's Indians had developed successful civilizations for a millennia before whites from any nation arrived. Oregon was not a wilderness to them, nor a frontier that needed pioneering, nor a land open to colonization by any foreign country. The Oregon pioneers of the 1840s and 1850s knew that to get their free land they would have to get rid of the Indians as well as the HBC, and they did so even more aggressively.[14] No defense can be made for the many atrocities inflicted by American pioneers on Oregon's Indians, but identifying the first among them serves a historical purpose, even if the designation is seen as an ignominious one by Oregon's native people.

If it had been up to Hall Kelley, American settlers would have pushed the HBC out of the way in 1832. Since 1817 he had worked to bring Oregon Country into the United States, and had come to believe the best way to accomplish that was to establish a permanent colony of American settlers. In 1824, while still an educator and textbook author, Kelley publicly announced plans to settle Oregon Country, and by 1829 he had dedicated himself to the endeavor full time. He established the American Society for Encouraging the Settlement of the Oregon Territory (American Society) and in 1831 began soliciting members through agents, advertisements, and circulars.[15]

In *A General Circular to All Persons of Good Character, Who Wish to Emigrate to the Oregon Territory,* Kelley laid out detailed plans for his colony in Oregon and described the kind of settler he was looking for: "The valley of the Multnomah will be occupied for agricultural and manufacturing operations, where likewise, a two mile square will be appropriated for a trading town" by "men of steady habits, virtuous intentions, endeavoring to cultivate practical knowledge and honest industry" and who would be "actuated by no other motives, than those of philanthropy and patriotism." Kelley was deeply religious and included a missionary component to his plans. He acknowledged Indian ownership of the land, but naively and incorrectly assumed that they would gladly trade their lands for Jesus, education, housing, training in farming, and other aspects of civilization after being exposed to them.[16]

Portrait of Hall Kelley, page 59 of *Oregon, Her History, Her Great Men, Her Literature,* by John B. Horner (1919).

Like many visionaries, Kelley was ahead of his time. The press ridiculed him, not enough people signed up, and Congress would not help out. Eventually, he gave up on the American Society.[17] That probably worked out for the best. Hundreds of American pioneers setting up camp just downstream from Fort Vancouver in 1832, fired up to oust the HBC while they were still seeing high profits from their Oregon Country operations, could have led to another war with Great Britain. Disease was starting to weaken the tribes along the Columbia River (because they had the most contact with whites) but it had not yet completely decimated them.[18] A large group of Americans settling on their lands could have caused a violent reaction. Fourteen years later Oregon Country became part of the United States without bloodshed.

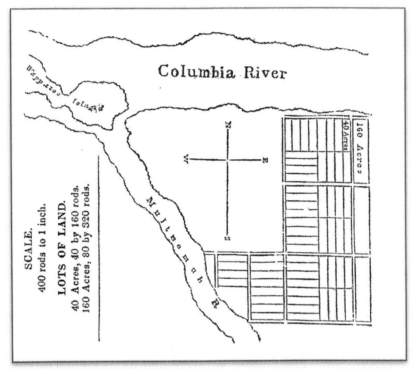

American settlement laid out by Hall Kelley, page 26 of his *A General Circular to All Persons of Good Character Who Wish to Emigrate to the Oregon Territory* (1831).

One of those who had signed on as an agent with Kelley was Nathaniel Wyeth. He was not interested in Kelley's vision of patriotic colonization, but saw the American Society as an expedient way to get to Oregon Country to carry out his own commercial plans to trap beaver and fish for salmon to ship back to Massachusetts. Wyeth's previous business success made him confident he could successfully compete with the HBC where others had failed. By the end of 1831 Wyeth had begun to doubt Kelley's ability to organize and lead anyone to Oregon Country,

Portrait of Nathaniel Wyeth, page 836 of *Harper's New Monthly Magazine* (November 1892)

and he objected strenuously to Kelley's decision to include families, so he set up the Pacific Trading Company and started recruiting on his own.[19]

After a couple months of meetings and ten days of training on Long Island (none of them—including Wyeth—had any wilderness experience), twenty-two Pacific Trading Company members left Boston Harbor by ship March 10, 1832. Four men joined them after landing in Baltimore. From there they headed overland by train, wagon, and horseback to Independence, Missouri, where William Sublette allowed them to join his supply train headed for the fur trapper's rendezvous being held at Pierre's Hole (Idaho) that year. Desertions began almost immediately. Living outdoors and overland travel was not as easy as it had sounded sitting around Wyeth's fireplace in Cambridge or the campfire on Long Island.[20] Fourteen of the twenty-six men eventually turned back, most of them at Pierre's Hole. Three of these men died before getting home.

1861 map cropped to show Long Island relative to Boston and Cambridge. Boston Public Library, G3762.B65 1861. E6.

After the rendezvous broke up, a group of mountain men, which Wyeth's group joined for the next part of their journey, got into a major battle with a band of Gros Ventres Indians. Wyeth wisely kept his greenhorns out of the fight, and they all made it to Fort Vancouver. However, one of them died soon after arriving, and two more died within four years.[21] Wyeth led a larger group of fifty men to Oregon Country in 1834. On September 22, 1835, he wrote his wife that he "had lost by drowning, disease, and warfare 17 persons up to this date, and 14 now sick."[22] Many pioneers would later die on the Oregon Trail, but they had nowhere near the 30% mortality rate of Wyeth's expeditions. Being first had its risks.

Though initially protesting the defection, Kelley eventually asked Wyeth to take three American Society members with him. Kelley's biographer, Fred Wilbur Powell, identified them: "J. Sinclair of New York; John Ball, a native of New Hampshire, practicing law in New York; Calvin Tibbetts [*Tibbets*], a native of Maine and by trade a stone-cutter."[23] All three of these men continued to Oregon, whereas only nine of the twenty-three men Wyeth recruited stuck it out.[24] This suggests that colonization was a more powerful driving force than the prospects of financial gain.

When Sinclair, Ball, and Tibbets transferred to Wyeth, it was to expedite their settlement in Oregon, as indicated in a letter John Sinclair wrote to Kelley: "What difference would it make to the Society, should I go to the Oregon country with Capt. Wyeth's party, if in the country when the expedition arrives."[25]

These men did not know then that Kelley would eventually abandon his colonization effort. They were just using Wyeth to get there more quickly. Since Kelley had been recruiting in the same market as Wyeth for a longer period of time, the assumption has to be made that the men who signed up with Wyeth were in it for profit rather than colonization. Sinclair's letter, along with American Society membership, establishes Ball, Sinclair, and Tibbets as the initial candidates for designation as Oregon's first pioneer, because they had signed up with Kelley, whose intent was colonization of Oregon, with the eventual end being American statehood.

Wyeth's enterprise failed within a month of arriving in Oregon Country because the ship he had sent to meet them there (the *Sultana*) had shipwrecked on a reef in the Society Islands in the southern Pacific Ocean. He was left with no supplies or items for trading with Indians, and no way to return furs and salmon to Boston.[26] So Wyeth released Calvin Tibbets and the other men from their contracts, saying "they were good men and persevered as long as perseverance would do good."[27] After arriving with his second expedition, another American fur company reneged on its earlier agreement with Wyeth, making it even more difficult to compete with the HBC. After four years of concerted effort, Nathaniel Wyeth gave up and returned to Cambridge.[28]

Wyeth was eventually recognized for having led the first permanent American settlers to Oregon, even though that was not his purpose. Historian Robert Clark called Wyeth's contribution "the wedge that eventually split the Hudson's Bay Company monopoly."[29] Matthew Deady (Oregon Territorial Supreme Court Judge and the first Federal District Court Judge of Oregon) appropriately expanded the credit to include Kelley: "This attempt of Wyeth's, which itself was largely a consequence of Kelley's scheme, was not without results conductive [*sic*] to American occupation. Divers [*sic*] persons employed in the enterprise remained in the country and were the beginning of the independent American settlers in the country."[30] Since neither Kelley nor Wyeth stayed in Oregon, it was up to men like Calvin Tibbets to drive that wedge in.

The first thing Tibbets and his cohorts did to pave the way for future Oregon pioneers was to finalize sections of the route they would take. In 1832 the Oregon Trail did not exist. Fur trappers had established a route following the Platte River and across the Rocky Mountains at South Pass in order to get to their annual rendezvous, but the route from the Rockies to Oregon was yet to be worked out. For the Oregon Trail to become what *Atlas of Oregon* authors called the "path of empire" by "opening the Oregon Country to occupation by pioneers and acquisition by the United States," someone had to fill in the gaps.[31]

In 1884 Hubert Howe Bancroft wrote that Wyeth's 1832 expedition "marked the way for the ox-teams which were so shortly to bring the Americanized civilization of Europe across the roadless continent."[32] Fifty years later Archer Hulbert wrote, "Before 1830 that track to the Rockies was not recognized as a highway to the Pacific, and prior to 1835 it would have been idle to try to persuade the public that women and children could, in one season, go comfortably from Atlantic

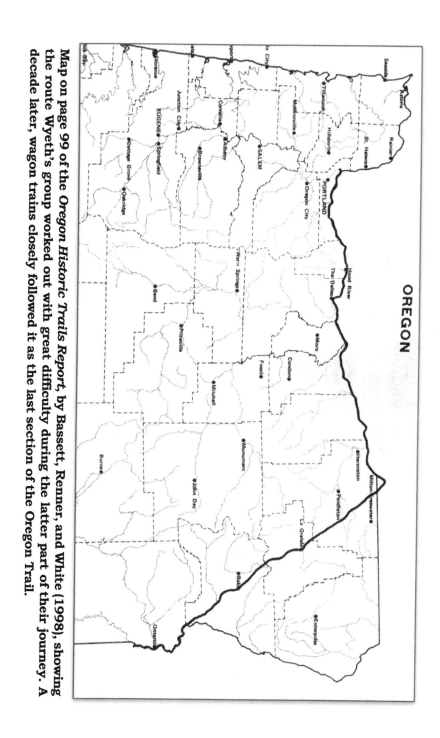

Map on page 99 of the *Oregon Historic Trails Report*, by Bassett, Renner, and White (1998), showing the route Wyeth's group worked out with great difficulty during the latter part of their journey. A decade later, wagon trains closely followed it as the last section of the Oregon Trail.

tide water *[sic]* to the Pacific." Of Wyeth's journal, Hulbert said, "It is the first account we have of the experiences of Americans traversing what became the historic Oregon-California trail across Nebraska, Wyoming, Idaho, and Oregon to the mouth of the Columbia."[33] In its 1998 report, the Oregon Trail Coordination Council described the route worked out by Wyeth's men as "the Oregon Trail as far as the Grande Rhonde Valley" and the "Whitman Trail over the western summits of the Blue Mountains." As to its significance: "Wyeth's initial trip in 1832 provided the foundation and experience for the 1834 trip. . . . Wyeth's route was as precursor to the Oregon Trail route followed by hundreds of thousands beginning just a decade later."[34]

In the spring of 1833, after wintering at Fort Vancouver, Calvin Tibbets and John Ball headed south to farm at Champoeg, with John Sinclair joining them at times.[35] This was the northern part of what came to be known as French Prairie, the area along the Willamette River between the modern cities of Salem and Newburg. Fur trapping brigades had traveled through the area going back to John Jacob Astor's failed Pacific Fur Company venture twenty years earlier, but HBC retirees had recently begun settling there permanently instead of returning to Canada.[36] So Ball, Tibbets, and Sinclair had arrived just in time to serve as American placeholders in Oregon Country's first permanent settlement.

Unfortunately, Ball and Sinclair only lasted one summer. The first three months, while building his own cabin, Ball stayed with Jean Baptiste Deportes McKay, who he described to a friend in a letter home as "a half-breed, with two wives, his name J.B. Deportes. Yes, two wives, seven children, and cats and dogs numberless." After the novelty of this wore off, Ball found himself unable to tolerate the

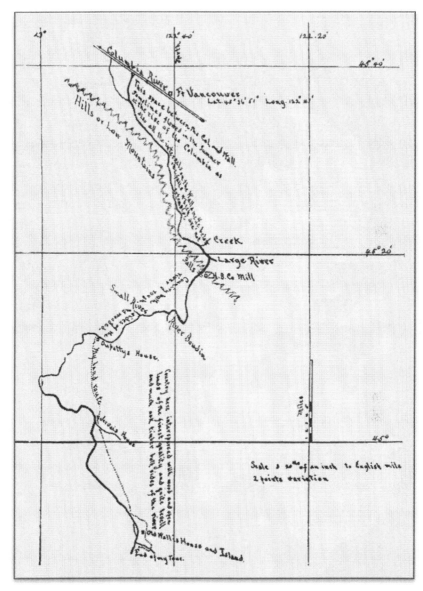

Map drawn by Nathaniel Wyeth in November 1832, showing the settled parts of Oregon Country, opposite page 178 of *Correspondence and Journals of Nathaniel J. Wyeth, 1831-1836,* **by F.G. Young (1899).**

rough ways of his French Canadian neighbors, and their intermarriage with Indians, long enough to wait for Kelley to
bring more civilized Americans with whom to associate.
Ball and Sinclair also suffered from malaria and saw the
devastating effect it had on neighboring Kalapuyan Indians.
With no physician close by, they had reason to fear for their
future well-being. So Ball and Sinclair booked passage on
the HBC's supply ship the *Dryad*, and set sail for home in
the middle of October 1833. Eventually Ball found the sort
of colonization he was looking for in the development of
Grand Rapids, Michigan, where he left a lasting legacy.[37] As
Fred Powell points out, after Ball and Sinclair left, "Calvin
Tibbetts [*Tibbets*] was the only man whose enrollment on
the books of the American Society was followed by emigra-
tion and settlement."[38]

Two other Americans remained in Oregon who had come
with Wyeth but were not members of the American Society.
Greely Sargent trapped for the HBC for a couple years, but
when he died in 1836 he was at the Willamette Methodist
Mission.[39] Solomon Smith taught the children at Fort Vancouver (John Ball had done so earlier) until the summer of
1834, when he left for French Prairie to live with Clatsop
princess Celiast (who he had met at Fort Vancouver) and to
teach the children of retired HBC employees, mostly French
Canadian. From 1836 to 1840 Smith helped build and oper-
ate a sawmill with Ewing Young. Then he moved to Clatsop
Plains, the coastal area between Seaside and Warrenton so
that Celiast could return to her people. The Methodists hired
him to help them build a mission there, with Calvin Tibbets
joining them to form the first settlement in Clatsop County.[40]

At this point Calvin Tibbets qualifies as Oregon's first
pioneer, but does he actually deserve to be recognized for
it? Being the last of Kelley's American Society standing
proves he was the first American to come to Oregon with

a stated intent to settle permanently, build an American colony, and make it part of the United States, but what did he do to carry out this intention?

Portrait of Solomon and Celiast (Helen) Smith. Oregon Historical Society (OHS), Call Number 014130.

When Powell wrote Kelley's biography, he knew that other Americans would eventually arrive in Oregon, and that it would become part of the United States, but in 1833 Tibbets did not. He likely had begun doubting that Kelley would show up with his colonists, and had no idea when others might come. To survive long enough to support them, if and when they did arrive, Tibbets would have to get along with his French Canadian neighbors, the HBC, and local Indians. This would require a more flexible personality, an adaptable belief system, and lower expectations than John Ball possessed.

Born the son of a farmer, Ball had worked his way through college to become an attorney and successful businessman. One result of his climbing the social ladder—evident in his writing—was a disdain for common laborers

COSTUME OF A CALLAPUYA INDIAN.

1841 sketch by Alfred Agate, member of the United States Exploring Expedition. OHS, OrHi 104921.

such as Tibbets, equal to that which he felt for his French Canadian neighbors.[41] Tibbets likely felt more at home. Though stonemasons are now considered middle class, in the early 1800s they were at the lower end of America's class structure. His stonemason skills, and the physical strength and acceptance of hard work the trade required, would have given Tibbets something more practical to trade than Ball's advanced education, legal skills, and business acumen. Being a lower class laborer increased Tibbets chances to survive in Oregon.

Fitting in would mean adopting the ways of his neighbors. There were no white women anywhere in Oregon Country when Calvin Tibbets arrived, but he would have noticed—as had John Ball—that his neighbors each had at least one Indian or métis wife. In addition to satisfying their basic need for companionship, employees of the HBC had learned that these "country marriages" were a key to survival and doing business among the tribes they traded with.[42]

The same benefits would have been obvious to Tibbets. He took up the practice, according to Rev. Jason Lee, who reported that on May 26, 1840, he "reached the lower part of the settlement, and about sunset set off on horseback for the mission. Night came on, and I slept at the house of Mrs. E. Tibbits [*Tibbets*]."[43] Whoever "Mrs. E" was, she had to have been Indian or métis, so their relationship shows Calvin Tibbets was more flexible than John Ball, and willing to adapt to a culture unlike his own.[44]

The HBC was the main force to be reckoned with if Tibbets was to survive in Oregon. Fort Vancouver was the only place to purchase supplies, typically trading them for wheat or furs, and HBC records show Tibbets did such trading.[45] He was invited on an inaugural run of the HBC's first

steamship, the *Beaver*, in 1836. Samuel Clarke reported
Willie McKay's description of the event in 1905:

> *He recollects it as one of the sunniest days in all
> his life - the happiest time he had any memory of.
> There were aboard McLoughlin, Douglas,
> McKinley and Work, and their families; also
> Pambrun, Missionary Samuel Parker, a com-
> panion of Whitman; John R. Thompson, of Phil-
> adelphia, the ornithologist; Calvin Tibbetts
> [Tibbets], James Gervais, E. Lucie and H. B. Em-
> ers. It was a distinguished party. So the* Beaver
> *made her trial trip, and for the first time a steam
> vessel ploughed the waters of the Columbia
> River.*[46]

This indicates Tibbets had gone beyond survival to earn
some measure of respect with the HBC within four years of
his arrival in Oregon Country.

**In the 1880s the *Beaver* served as a private cargo vessel. This
photo shows it hauling dry goods and cattle, working out of
Victoria, British Columbia. Clatsop County Historical Society,
Image # 4467.340.**

Calvin Tibbets did not have to wait long for more Americans to join him. In October 1834 Methodist missionaries Jason Lee and Daniel Lee (Jason's nephew), with lay assistants Cyrus Shepard and P. L. Edwards, arrived to start a mission at the southern end of French Prairie.[47] Tibbets was Congregationalist, another religion with missionary efforts, so he likely offered whatever assistance he could.[48]

Drawing of the Methodist mission on the Willamette River in 1834, opposite page 118 of Gaston's *Centennial History of Oregon 1.*

Jason Lee had felt comfortable enough to stay at Tibbets home when he was not there, and when Rev. Joseph Frost passed through on his way to the mission September 29, 1841, Tibbets loaned him a horse.[49] When the Methodists formed Oregon's first temperance society in 1836, Tibbets signed on, and he did the same later with Presbyterians on Clatsop Plains.[50] This gives some evidence that Tibbets believed in the missionary aspect of the American Society.

Missionaries mostly failed in their goal of Christianizing Indians. However, they had an important role in bringing American wagon train pioneers to Oregon. After their first mission was established, the Methodists sent more missionaries, including women, and eventually entire families. These missionaries wrote letters home to family and religious journals speaking of the moderate climate and fertile valleys of Oregon.[51] Kelley had been correct in thinking American families could survive in Oregon, but someone had to prove it before most families would be willing to take the chance.

While the Methodists were busy constructing their mission on the Willamette, another group of Americans were on their way to Oregon, this time from California. Hall Kelley was to finally make it to Oregon, sans American Society colonists. He had left Boston nearly two years earlier, traveled a difficult, circuitous route across Mexico, losing all his possessions to the authorities along the way. In California, Kelley managed to convince Ewing Young, an experienced American fur trapper, to lead him to Oregon. Kelley became so ill with malaria on the trip that Michel LaFramboise (leader of the HBC trappers who were competing with Young in California but happened to encounter them on the way back) took pity on him, administered some quinine, and got him back to Fort Vancouver

1855 drawing by Gustav Sohon, cropped to the original Fort Vancouver built by HBC (bird's-eye view from the northwest). Library of Congress Control Number (LCCN) 2011647869. Hall Kelley would have stayed in one of the outbuildings.

ahead of the rest of the group. There Kelley was nursed back to health, but in a cabin outside the fort. He felt isolated and disrespected by the HBC and fellow Americans alike, so after four months he left on the next ship out, never to return. But he continued to lobby for American acquisition of Oregon Country at home.[52] Though considered a failure by most, Kelley deserves credit for bringing both Calvin Tibbets and Ewing Young to Oregon.

Ewing Young, like Nathaniel Wyeth, was a man of action. Once in Oregon he established a fifty square mile ranch, "the standard size of a 'squatter's claim' by New Mexican and Californian standards," on Tualatin Plains, where he ran his horses, grew wheat, built a sawmill, operated a store, and hired men to work for him. The *Oregon Trails Historic Trails Report* noted, "His profit margins and extraordinary bookkeeping endeared him to the growing population of Americans, who entrusted their precious money with him, gradually establishing Young as a banker of sorts."[53] Finally an American who could successfully compete with the HBC had arrived in Oregon Country.

Oregon's first banker was not always flush with cash. In 1837 Ewing Young borrowed $12 from Calvin Tibbets to pay some debts, and after his death in 1841 his estate paid Tibbets $23. In today's dollars the figures would be $307 and $644, respectively.[54] Though not a great deal of money, it shows that the man Americans most trusted with their money in Oregon had a close enough relationship with Calvin Tibbets to know he had the money to lend, and felt comfortable asking him for it. It also shows that Tibbets was able and willing to assist in the financial health of the American community in Oregon.

In January 1837 Navy Lt. William Slacum traveled to Oregon Country on assignment from President Andrew Jackson. He visited the HBC, Indians, and settlers, and

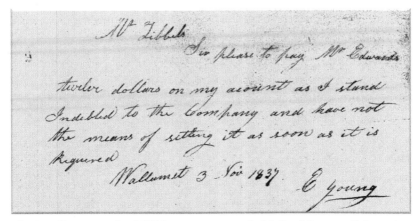

Ewing Young asked Tibbets to pay a debt for him on this note from the "Ewing Young Account Book." OHS, MSS 499.

returned to file a report that December.[55] And he did much more than that. In the spring of 1838 Slacum and Rev. Jason Lee presented what historian Cornelius Brosnan described as "the 'Oregon memorial of 1838,' the first formal expression from resident Oregonians for an American Oregon" to the United States Congress. It was signed by thirty-six men, including Calvin Tibbets. In public presentations, Slacum and Lee argued that Oregon would be a good addition to the United States, and that Americans in Oregon were in need of legal protection that the United States government owed them as citizens.[56]

As James Kelly (a Chief Justice of the Oregon Supreme Court and pioneer of 1851) explained the situation to the Oregon Pioneer Association in 1882, the French Canadian settlers were protected by British law administered through the HBC, and the missionaries were subject to church governance; however, many American citizens fit into neither category. Kelly said these men "were known in the community as independent settlers" and that because of the need for the rule of law they became the driving force toward statehood. The memorial and pleas of Lee and Slacum were not sufficient to move Congress to action. After several more years of being ignored by the Unites States Congress, and facing the need to deal with Ewing Young's estate, these independent settlers finally took matters into their own hands by forming Oregon's provisional government.[57]

While in Oregon Country, Lt. Slacum also helped American settlers fulfill their greatest need:

> *In the course of conversation with Mr. Lee, Young, and other settlers, I found that nothing was wanting to insure comfort, wealth, and every happiness to the people of this most beautiful country but the possession of neat cattle, all of those in the country being owned by the Hudson Bay Company, who refuse to sell them under any circumstances whatever.*[58]

When Ewing Young suggested they could buy cattle cheap in California and herd them back to Oregon, Slacum offered help with funding along with free transportation on his ship, the *Loriot*. Settlers set up the Willamette Cattle Company and set sail, with Calvin Tibbets subscribed and on board. Of this operation Slacum said, "The men are all experienced woodsmen. I certainly view this measure as one of the highest importance to the future growth and prosperity of this fine country, even if no other object is attained by my visit to the Columbia."[59] This was the first cattle drive of its kind in the United States, taking place twenty-five years before the more famous cattle drives that ran north from Texas across the Great Plains.[60]

Ewing Young traveled back and forth across California, and bargained hard with Mexican officials, to purchase 729 (mostly) wild longhorns. They proved difficult to gather and hold. The men struggled three weeks just to get them

406

Oregon Territory, Wallamette Settlement

Articles of Agreement made and entered into
this 13 th day of January in the Year of Our Lord One
Thousand Eight Hundred and Thirty Seven
Whereas, We the Undersigned Settlers upon the
Wallamette River, are fully convinced of the Importance
and Necessity of having Cattle of our own in order success-
=fully to carry on our farms and gain a comfortable
livelihood, And whereas We find it impossible to
purchase them here, as all the Cattle in the country
belong to the Hudsons Bay Company, and they refusing
to sell them under any circumstances, And as we
believe that the possession of Cattle will not only bene-
=fit us personally, but will materially benefit the whole
settlement, We the Undersigned do therefore Agree
1st To avail ourselves of an offer of Mr Slacum Esq
to take passage in the American Brig Loriot Capt
Bancroft, free of charge, to proceed to California to
purchase cattle for ourselves and all our Neighbors
who choose to join us in our Enterprise either
by accompanying us themselves or furnishing the
means of purchasing Cattle in California
2 We agree to furnish funds according to our
Means making a common stock concern subject
to the following conditions,
——— The expenses of all those who go down to California
are to be borne by the Company calculating the time
so employed at the rate of twenty dollars per Month;
provisions likewise to be paid by the company.
3d The wages of the men thus employed to be calculated
as so much money, and each one is to be credited
accordingly; and each and every member of the
Company shall have his portion of the cattle

The Wallamette [*Willamette*] Cattle Company Articles of Agreement. Oregon State Archives (OSA), Provisional Document 406.

which may arrive safely at the Wallamette, there to
be divided agreable to the capital and wages employed
in the enterprise.

4? All those who go for the purpose aforesaid to
California hereby bind themselves to return to the
Wallamette with the cattle and to use their best
endeavours to protect the same

5? We hereby agree that Ewing Young shall be
leader of the party and P. L. Edwards Treasu-
rer, And they shall be joint purchasers of the
Cattle

6? If any man shall desert the company in
California He shall forfeit all wages which he
may have earned

7? If after the arrival of the party in California
any man shall choose to labor for his personal
benefit he shall have liberty to do so —
provided — that he shall be bound to invest
the proceeds in the common stock, and
that he shall not enter into any engagements which
shall prevent him from leaving when required.
But such person shall not be entitled to any
remuneration from the Company for the
time so employed

Ewing Young   Calvin Tibbets

P L Edwards   Lawrence Carmichael

James A O'Neal   Pierre x Depau
                                        his mark
John x Turner   George Gay
      his mark
Wedley P Fauxhurst   William J Bailey
                               Emat x Laquette
                                        his mark

**This is the oldest record at OSA, dated January 13, 1837.
Tibbets' signature indicates the correct spelling of his name.**

across the San Joaquin River. Then one of the men, George Gay, killed a friendly Indian in the Shasta Valley and tensions rose within the group. Young had to apply a firm hand to resolve them. A fight with Rogues near the mouth of Foots Creek left several of the Americans wounded and at least a dozen Indians dead, but when they finally arrived home with 630 cows they had broken the HBC monopoly on cattle in Oregon.[61] By signing Slacum's memorial and participating in the cattle drive, Calvin Tibbets showed that the positive relationship he had built with the HBC was not going to detract from his ultimate goal of making Oregon part of the United States.

The wild Californian cattle that meant so much to the first Americans in Oregon were later slaugthered en masse just for their hides—like bison on the Great Plains.[74] This 1875 trade card shows how the leather made from both species were used to sell shoes. LCCN 9351160.

In 1838 Tibbets attempted to obtain more cattle from California with another group of nine Americans and eight Indians and métis. This time the Rogues turned them back. One man was killed on the spot, two died of their wounds in the Umpqua Mountains while in retreat, and Tibbets was severely wounded in the arm. He reported this to members of the United States Exploring Expedition (Expedition) while guiding and hunting for them when traveling from the Willamette Valley to San Francisco during September and October of 1841. Lt. George Foster Emmons, the group's leader, reported in his diary that since the successful 1837 cattle drive, "several attempts have been made to get up another party but without success." Titian Peale, Expedition naturalist, named the place where Indians most often ambushed whites "Bloody Pass." [62] The fact that Americans kept trying to get through Bloody Pass, regardless of the risks, confirms how important cattle were to them. The fact that Indians and métis went with them indicates that the Americans saw their support as critical.

A few months prior to the Expedition arriving in Oregon Country, Calvin Tibbets had moved to the mouth of the Columbia River to help Solomon Smith and the reverends Joseph Frost and William Kone set up a Methodist mission there.[63] The timing was fortunate for the crew of the *Peacock,* an Expedition ship, when it wrecked on the spit that now bears its name attempting to cross the Columbia Bar July 18, 1841.[64] Rev. Kone was preaching at the nearby Clatsop village that Sunday when one of his congregation (perhaps not paying as much attention as Kone would have liked) saw the ship and called it to their attention. As they watched the *Peacock,* they could see it was in trouble, so the Clatsops paddled Kone, Frost, and Tibbets over to Baker's Bay on the opposite (north) shore of the Columbia. There they provided food, fire, and shelter to the sailors, all of whom survived, including Lt. Emmons.[65]

Emmons crossed to Astoria the next day and found orders waiting for him from Lt. Charles Wilkes, Expedition commander, to lead a group to explore the interior of Oregon. Having become acquainted with Tibbets at the Baker's Bay camp, Emmons asked Wilkes' second-in-command,

Lt. William Hudson, to add him to the list of guides for the trip.[66] First Tibbets had to finish guiding James Dana, Expedition geologist, to the top of Saddle Mountain, the highest peak in the Coast Range. This was its first recorded ascent by whites.[67]

When Tibbets caught up with Emmons, he found the lieutenant in a tough spot. His lead guide, Jean Baptiste Deportes McKay (John Ball's host), had quit due to a severe attack of malaria.[68] Joe Meek, Robert Newell, William Craig, George Ebbert, and Caleb Wilkens, all of whom had originally contracted with Wilkes, backed out when he sent new orders for Emmons to continue down through northern California and meet the squadron at San Francisco rather than return to the Willamette.

Reports had been received that Rogues and Shastas were lying in wait for the group, so Emmons was sorry to lose these experienced Indian fighters. They explained that they had families to care for and crops to bring in, and that leaving so late in the year meant they would have to stay in California until the spring when the passes were clear of snow. They would also have to wait to get together a group large enough to make it safely back through Bloody Pass. Emmons eventually accepted this, but finding replacements was difficult.[69]

Meek and the others also would have realized that they had no experience with the route or Indians of Southern Oregon and Northern California, whereas Calvin Tibbets and others who had been in Oregon longer did. They also would have known that the best chance of getting back to Oregon safely was to join an HBC brigade returning from winter trapping. Having been bitter enemies of the HBC while trapping in the Rockies, that would have been untenable for them, whereas Tibbets and other Americans had a good relationship with the HBC.

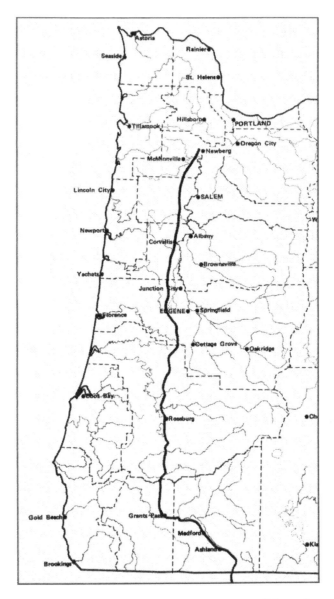

On page 129 of Bassett et al.'s *Oregon Historic Trails Report*, this map is identified as the "Ewing Young Route," but associated text explains that it was established by HBC fur brigades. It would have been used by the Emmons group and anyone else traveling through Oregon during that era.

Among those Emmons found to replace Meek and the other retired mountain men were Indian and métis men and women, which was fortuitous. When the group got lost south of Mt. Shasta, it was Lisette—métis wife of James Warfield—

who got them back on track by locating rocks she had placed in strategic places while traveling through the area previously. [70] Warfield was one of those who had taken advantage of Emmons' situation by a demand for higher wages and

Drawing of Mt. Shasta by Alfred Agate, opposite page 240 of *Narrative of the Exploring Expedition, Volume V*, by Charles Wilkes (1849).

payment for their trip back. Emmons was clearly irritated by this: "The fickleness of my men giving me much trouble. Tibbets and Black only remaining steadfast." Perhaps out of appreciation, Emmons named a creek after Tibbets.[71]

When Emmons asked Josiah Whitcomb, the Methodist mission farmer, if he could borrow his bulldog because of its reputation for chasing off Indians, Whitcomb agreed, but only after being assured that his dog would be kept under Tibbet's care and brought back. Emmons reported difficulty restraining this beast from attacking the friendly Indians they met along the way, so it may have been a factor in their making it safely past Bloody Pass and all the way to San Francisco without incident. Another likely factor was the size and makeup of the group: twenty-eight armed men, accompanied by eleven women and children, showed unfriendly Indians that they had peaceful intentions but would make any attackers pay dearly.[72]

When Calvin Tibbets returned to Clatsop Plains in September of 1842 he was driving a herd of cattle with the help of Peter Brainard, an American he had recruited for the task in California.[73] One reason it took nearly a year was that—unlike 1837—cattle were scarce and expensive. Hunters had been killing them just for their hides, which were fetching high prices. Through the winter and spring Tibbets and the other Americans either worked for John Sutter or trapped beaver with the HBC brigade led by Francis Ermatinger. This would have supplemented the wages they received from Emmons and helped them buy more cattle.[74] Tibbets and some of the other Americans joined the HBC brigade in late spring of 1842 to return home safely.[75] The risk and effort was evidently worth it because Francis Fuller Victor said Tibbets' cattle "added much to the prosperity of that portion of the country."[76]

Solomon Smith or William Raymond (a lay Methodist who joined the Clatsop mission in July 1842) must have told Victor about the immediate economic impact of Tibbets' cattle, because Tibbets did not live long enough to do so himself, and the missionaries he had helped to set up the mission were gone. Rev. Kone and his family had returned to America on the *Columbia* in November 1841. Rev. Frost and his family left on the *Diamond* in August 1843. Both Kone and Frost were discouraged by the Clatsops' lack of interest in Christianity and appalled by some aspects of their culture, such as slavery. Though most of the Clatsops were friendly and helpful, they were not always dependable, and occasionally violent. In addition, members of the missionary families were persistently ill, and doctors distant.[77]

Taking a break from farming, Tibbets and Smith traveled to Champoeg for a meeting on May 2, 1843, where they voted with the majority in favor of creating a provisional government.[78] The event evidently inspired Tibbets to do some personal recruiting. In 1936 Albert Tozier (longtime caretaker of Champoeg) told *Oregon Journal* writer Fred Lockley:

> *Calvin Tibbets, associated with John Ball in farming here in 1833, was first cousin of my father's mother. He wrote a letter to Grandfather Tozier, which curiously enough, was dated May 2, 1843 – the very day that the provisional government was formed in Oregon. Tibbets was present at this meeting and voted for the provisional government. In this letter he said that if the United States ever took possession of the Oregon Country it would pay Grandfather to come to the Willamette Valley, as it was one of the most productive and finest countries he had ever seen.*[79]

Tibbets sent additional letters that "kindled anew the interest taken in the Oregon Country. The family from Maine and the family from Indiana brought with them a collection of books, papers and clippings relating the Oregon Country."[80] Tibbets' cousin did not arrive until 1862, and Tozier's family not until 1863, both long after Tibbets' death, so there would be no family reunion.[81] But his recruiting showed a continuing effort to make the American colony in Oregon grow.

As the Frost family was sailing home in the fall of 1843, the first American pioneers of the covered wagon era were on their way to Clatsop Plains.[82] Tibbets was surely pleased to see them and ready to lend a hand. He went so far as to take some of them into his home until they had built their own, namely A.C. Wirt, Fernando Swezey, and Richard Hobson.[83] After seeing his missionary friends leave, Tibbets was likely more determined than ever to do what he could to make sure Americans who came to Oregon stayed.

Drawing of Joe Meek calling for a vote at Champoeg on May 2, 1843, opposite page 160 of Gaston's *Centennial History of Oregon 1*. Some of those present (not Tibbets) are realistically depicted and identified at http://www.gegoux.com/boo-map.html.

One thing new settlers found missing upon arrival at Clatsop Plains was a gristmill. They had used coffee grinders along the trail, but as Warrenton historian Lyle Anderson quipped, "That was mostly pastime. Now the days weren't long enough."[84] Preston Gillette (*Oregonian* contributor and early settler himself) told the story of William Hobson as an example of the extremes settlers would go through to get their wheat ground. After the harvest of 1844, Hobson loaded up a canoe with sacks of wheat and had his son John and George Summers paddle it to a new commercial mill at Willamette Falls. When it capsized, the boys managed to retrieve some of the wet sacks and "took one to Oregon City, procured a vacant room over a kitchen, spread their wheat out on the floor and kept a big fire in the stove below until it was dry enough to grind. It took them about two weeks to make this trip."[85] Clearly, Clatsop Plains needed its own gristmill.

In 1845 Calvin Tibbets, William Perry, Thomas Owens, Edward Williams, and Elbridge Trask formed the Wahoni Milling Company and built a gristmill at the south end of Clatsop Plains near the mouth of the Neawanna River. The Oregon Provisional House of Representatives passed a special law incorporating the business on behalf of the owners, who wanted to make sure the land would not be claimed by new settlers.[86] In this case, Tibbets helped Oregon pioneers thrive by giving them a way to put bread on their tables.

Some of the new American arrivals disapproved of one way in which Calvin Tibbets had adapted to survive in Oregon long enough to be there to help them when they arrived. In 1843 Tibbets entered into another country marriage, this time with a Clatsop Indian whose English name was Louisa. They had two children: Grace in 1845 and John in 1846.[87] While earlier Americans in Oregon like Tibbets had come primarily from New England (Indians commonly referred to all whites as "Boston men"), wagon train pioneers were predominantly from the South and Midwest. Many were racist and intolerant of white intermarriage with Indians and métis.[88]

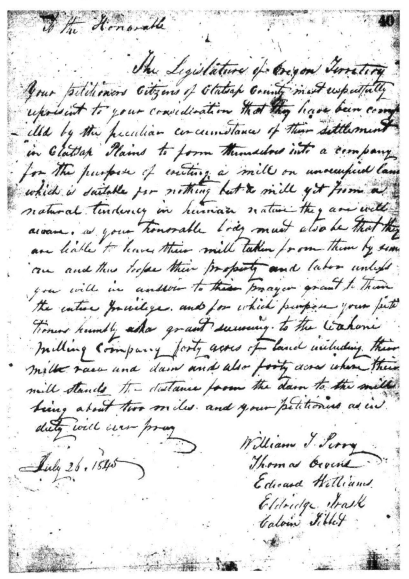

Wahoni Milling Company letter requesting legislative protection, July 26, 1845. OSA, Provisional Document 40.

Colonel John Adair (son of Astoria's first customs official and second husband of Dr. Bethenia Owens-Adair) recalled such bias among his Astorian neighbors: "Shively and Welch looked down on McClure because he had married an Indian woman."[89] Coveting the land claims of métis and whites married to Indians exacerbated some pioneers' bigotry. In 1845 John McLoughlin reported that "some of the Immigrants last come have said that every man who has an Indian wife ought to be driven out of the Country, and that the half breeds should not be allowed to hold lands."[90]

At his estate probate hearings, neighbors testified that Tibbets had told them he would not bring Louisa to public meetings when he knew white wives would be there. But he also said that he would not "turn her off," a phrase HBC officers used for the practice of leaving their Indian or métis wives behind when they returned to civilization.[91] Perhaps Tibbets viewed those of his American neighbors who were racist as a means to the end of Oregon becoming part of the United States that he just had to live with.

In addition to racism and disease, the Clatsop Indians suffered from abuse of liquor that unscrupulous whites used as a medium of trade in order to get the better of them. Historians Robert Ruby and John Brown judged that "their plight might have been worse had Clatsop country churchmen Solomon Smith, Calvin Tibbits [*Tibbets*], and W. H. Gray . . . not labored on their behalf."[92] William Gray originally came to Oregon Country as part of Rev. Marcus Whitman's Presbyterian mission. After settling near Tibbets and Smith in 1846 he helped form the Clatsop Plains Pioneer Presbyterian Church.

Tibbets joined an association that church trustees created in the summer of 1847 to combat the illegal sale of liquor to Indians.[93] They soon went after George Geer, who had been run out of Oregon for selling liquor to the

Clatsops in 1842 and was back at it again.[94] After helping to capture Geer, Tibbets served as presiding judge at the trial. The jury found Geer guilty and fined him $166.[95]

Early in 1849 Tibbets gave the Clatsop Plains Presbyterian Church five acres at the south end of his provisional land claim where they could build a church and cemetery.[96] Until then, they had been holding services in the homes of William Gray and Robert Morrison. After

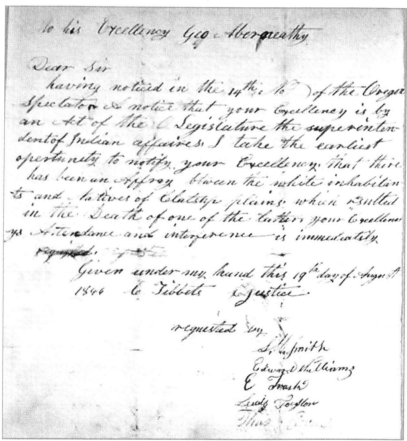

On August 19, 1846, District Judge Calvin Tibbets wrote to George Abernathy, Oregon Provisional Governor and Superintendent of Indian Affairs, informing him that a Clatsop Indian had been killed by a white settler. OHS, MSS 929. Tibbets described the details of this event in a letter to the editor of the *Oregon Spector* September 9, 1846.

a sailor's body washed ashore and a man was accidently shot, they felt the need to establish a cemetery for Christian burial. And of course a cemetery required a church. This historic congregation still serves the community, though no plaque or document acknowledges Tibbets' contribution to its earliest days.[97]

As the church was being built, most of Oregon's male population headed for the gold mines of California. Oregon had been in an economic depression since 1847, so this was an opportunity that was hard to pass up.[98] Calvin Tibbets and three neighbors he had worked with on the Wahoni Mill (Elbridge Trask, Thomas Owens, and William Perry) figured out how to make money off the gold discovery without leaving their families: by building a ship, filling it

The *Pioneer*, built by Tibbets and his neighbors, had a design similar to the *Morning Star*, built later by Tillamook settlers. This photo of its replica, the *Morning Star II*, is in Axel Anderson's album at the Tillamook County Pioneer Museum (TCPM). Another replica is at the Tillamook Cheese Factory.

with their farm produce, sailing it to California, and selling both the ship and produce at inflated prices. The experience Tibbets gained traveling to and from California with Lt. Slacum in 1837 and Lt. Emmons in 1841 would have been invaluable, but they needed someone who knew how to build and pilot a ship, so they recruited Robert MacEwan with notices placed in the *Oregon Free Press* dur-

Photo of Elbridge Trask, a neighbor of Tibbets who later moved to Tillamook. TCPM.

ing the fall of 1848. That winter they built a sixty-ton, two-masted schooner at Skipanon Landing (which was on the west bank of the Skipanon River in today's Warrenton) and called it the *Pioneer*.[99]

When they set sail for San Francisco June 16, 1849, Fernando Swazey had taken the place of Trask, probably because he was a blacksmith whose skills would come in handy keeping the ship together en route.[100] Dr. Bethenia Owens-Adair, who was the daughter of Thomas Owens and present at the launch, thought the *Pioneer* was "crude in the extreme. No experienced mariner would have wanted to put to sea in it, but Owens and his neighbors were accustomed to putting up with makeshifts, so they loaded their homemade schooner with bacon, pickled salmon, cabbage, potatoes, hides, hemlock bark and cranberries and put to sea to go to the newly discovered gold fields in California . . . and sold their cargo at top prices."[101] On another occasion, Owens-Adair recalled the launch being "a great day for Clatsop, everyone was there, including the Indians. They came in wagons, a horse back *[sic]* and on foot. The visitors from Astoria came in sailboats, row boats *[sic]* and canoes."[102]

One of the Astoria visitors was General John Adair, who had just arrived to serve as U.S. Collector of Customs for the newly established Oregon Territory.[103] Departure of the *Pioneer* was one of his first journal entries, and his recognition of the significance of the event is indicated by the details he included—unlike other ships—such as the names of all on board.[104]

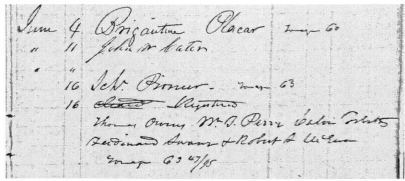

U.S. Customs log entry for the *Pioneer*, listing Tibbets and fellow crew members. Volume 1, Entrances and Clearances, Collection District of Astoria, RG 036, National Archives and Records Administration – Seattle.[100]

Calvin Tibbets was not with his fellow mariner-farmers when they arrived home on board the *Anita* August 11, 1849. He had died of cholera on the trip back, and had been buried at sea.[105] Given the high mortality rate among Wyeth's men, and many other risks Tibbets had taken since arriving in Oregon, he had survived longer than might be expected. Best of all, he had lived long enough to see his dream of Oregon Country becoming part of the Unites States come true. And his last project again benefited his fellow American settlers: Hannah Pease, who moved to Skipanon Landing a year after the *Pioneer* was built, recalled that the profits "brought a great deal of money into Clatsop."[106]

The settling of Tibbets' estate would have been a boon to the local economy as well. The total value came to about $7000 ($224,000 adjusted for inflation).[107] This was no mean achievement for a stonemason who had left Maine with nothing seventeen years earlier. It was more than his friend Ewing Young's estate had settled for.[108] Louisa died soon after Calvin, and much of the estate funds were paid to families who cared for John and Grace.[109]

The common way to deal with orphans at the time was to indenture them to families for whom they would work until adulthood in return for food, housing, and clothes.[110] Tibbets' hard-earned wealth spared his children that fate. It also enabled Grace to attend the Young Ladies Boarding School and Day School, run by the Sisters of Notre Dame De Namur, in Oregon City.[111] This would have pleased Tibbets, for in his final days on the *Anita*, he had asked Robert MacEwan to "take his daughter Grace and attend to her education." Solomon Smith reported that Tibbets wanted his son John educated also, but there is no indication that he attended school. In fact, no mention of John has been found after his father's estate closed in 1854.[112]

After her school closed in 1853, Grace continued to live with Robert Caufield's family in Oregon City, where she had stayed while attending the school.[113] In 1877 she married Richard Sorter, a black pioneer of 1858. Likely due to racial intolerance in Oregon, Grace and Richard moved to Kalama, Washington, to raise their family.[114] For the same reason, it is unlikely she ever attended Oregon Pioneer Association (OPA) meetings, so would not have heard members reminisce about her father. Grace was only four years old when her father died, so her own memory of him would have been limited. Grace probably lived her life unaware of the part her father played in making Oregon part of the United States.

Photo of Richard and Grace (Tibbets) Sorter, provided by descendants Oscar Moody and Daniel Kukkonen.

Even if Grace Tibbets had attended OPA meetings, she would have heard the story of her father's life told in bits and pieces. Many of Tibbets' contemporaries mentioned him to historians over the years, but they could speak only of the part of his life they were involved in, like the blind men describing an elephant in the ancient parable. [115] Calvin Tibbets' impact on Oregon history was a cumulative one that can only be appreciated when presented as a whole—as done here.

Calvin Tibbets would have had no impact on Oregon history if he had not first been captivated by Hall Kelley's vision of colonizing Oregon Country with Americans. When Kelley faltered, he joined Nathaniel Wyeth, left his urban life in Maine, and learned how to hunt for food, live outdoors, ride a horse, paddle a canoe, trap beaver, and fight hostile Indians. He endured hunger, illness, and other physical and emotional hardships of life in the wild. Once in Oregon, Tibbets persevered to become the only member of Kelley's American Society to remain permanently. In doing so, he was the first American to travel to Oregon with the stated intent of settling permanently and making it part of the United States.

Having met this definition of Oregon's first pioneer, Tibbets went on to earn recognition for it by doing everything he could in the remaining seventeen years of his life to pave the way for fellow American settlers, who—when they finally came in sufficient numbers—were able to wrest control of Oregon from Great Britain. It is time for an American to be named Oregon's first pioneer, and Calvin Tibbets is the best choice.

Notes

1. Frederic G. Young, ed., *The Correspondence and Journals of Captain Nathaniel J. Wyeth, 1831-36*, (Eugene, Ore: University Press, 1899), 176-177.

2. Stephen Dow Beckham, "Notable Oregonians: John McLoughlin-Father of Oregon," *Oregon Blue Book*, http://bluebook.state.or.us/notable/notmcloughlin.htm (accessed June 3, 2016); E.E. Rich, ed., *The Letters of John McLoughlin from Fort Vancouver to the Governor and Committee: First Series, 1825-38* (Toronto: The Champlain Society, 1941), 108-109.

3. Before the Unites States Congress created the Oregon Territory in 1848, "Oregon," "Oregon Country," and "Oregon Territory" were used interchangeably (mostly by Americans) for the vast area that ran from the Continental Divide to the Pacific Ocean, and from the northern edge of Mexico's claims at the 42nd parallel to the southern edge of Russia's claims at 54'40". This included all of the modern states of Oregon, Washington, and Idaho; the western parts of Montana and Wyoming; and most of the province of British Columbia. During the Convention of 1818, the United States and Great Britain agreed to the 49th parallel as the northern boundary of shared jurisdiction, but many Americans continued arguing for 54'40" throughout the decades of dispute; so it is shown as the greatest extent on most maps. This broader boundary of Oregon Country closely matched that of the Columbia District of the North West Company in 1818, and the HBC after 1821, when Great Britain forced the two companies to merge. HBC then moved from Fort George (Astoria) to Fort Vancouver. See a collection of maps of Oregon Country, spanning three and a half centuries, at: James Walker, "Cartography of Oregon, 1507-1848," *Oregon Encyclopedia*, http://oregonencyclopedia.org/articles/cartography_of_oregon_1507_1848/#.V1NGMHn2YWw. Unfortunately, none of these historical maps clearly depict the boundaries of Oregon Country. The map placed opposite the first page was created by Washington, D.C. cartographer, Karl Musser: *Wikimedia Commons*, https://commons.wikimedia.org/wiki/File%3AOregoncountry.png (accessed June 4, 2016).

4. Young, *Journals of Wyeth*, xiv-xvii; Richard White, *It's Your Misfortune and None of My Own: A New History of the American West* (Norman: University of Oklahoma Press, 1991), 69-71; Gregory P.

Shine, "Hudson's Bay Company," *The Oregon Encyclopedia*, http://or-egonencyclopedia.org/articles/hudson_s_bay_company/#.V1IH-Gnn2Z5w (accessed June 3, 2016); Frederick Merk, *The Oregon Question: Essays in Anglo-American Diplomacy and Politics* (Cambridge: Belknap Press of Harvard University Press, 1967), 172.

5. Young, *Journals of Wyeth*, xvi; White, *Misfortune*, 73-76.

6. Merk, *Oregon Question*, xii-xiii, 244-254.

7. Stephen Dow Beckham, "Oregon History: Land-based Fur Trade and Exploration," *Oregon Blue Book*, http://www.bluebook.state.or.us/cultural/history/history06.htm (accessed June 3, 2016).

8. Stephen Dow Beckham, "Oregon History: The 'Oregon Question' and Provisional Government," *Oregon Blue Book*, http://www.bluebook.state.or.us/cultural/history/history10.htm (accessed June 3, 2016). The American pioneers were of course unaware of the positions of the American and British negotiators. One of the reasons the Applegate Trail was established was to provide Americans a safer route to travel between Oregon and the United States if war broke out. This was in 1846, the same year the Oregon Question was answered: Jeff LaLande, "Applegate Trail," *Oregon Encyclopedia*, http://oregonencyclopedia.org/articles/applegate_trail/#.V1IJX3n2Z5w (accessed June 4, 2016).

9. Based on a search of several internet search engines, JSTOR, HathiTrust, Google, Google Books, Google Scholar, Archive.org, and Worldcat, using the phrases "Oregon's first pioneer," "first Oregon pioneer," and "first pioneer of Oregon."

10. "Short Notices," *The Geographical Journal* 31, no. 4 (1908): 438.

11. McLoughlin became an American citizen after leaving the HBC, but that was long after he could have been considered a pioneer. Some historians have suggested that his benevolence was not entirely out of personal kindness. He justified his actions with superiors by saying that he aided American settlers because if he had not, they would have pillaged the forts along the Oregon Trail as well as in Oregon Country. Americans had a negative view of despots, benevolent or not, so many had a hard time feeling thankful to McLoughlin. Many despised him: Leslie M. Scott, "Influence of American Settlement Upon the Oregon Boundary Treaty of 1846" *Oregon Historical Quarterly* 29, no. 1 (March 1928): 17-19. In 1957 the Oregon State Legislature concluded that McLoughlin had been mistreated by his contemporary Oregonians and attempted to make up for this by taking up Holman's theme: they named him the "Father of Oregon" and had his statue displayed on the

state's behalf in Washington, D. C.: Beckham, "McLoughlin - Father of Oregon."

12. William G. Robbins, *Landscapes of Promise: The Oregon Story, 1800-1940* (Seattle: University of Washington Press, 1997), 83.

13. In addition to the strong connotation associated with "Oregon pioneer," narrowing the use of "pioneer" to those who first ventured to a region new to them, with the intent to "settle" permanently and "colonize" it on behalf of their home country, is supported by the discussion of each of these terms as they are presented progressively in the *Merriam-Webster Online Dictionary*: *http://www.merriam-webster. com* (accessed June 3, 2016).

14. See note 12 above. As will be shown, Calvin Tibbets had a much different attitude towards Oregon's Indians than the American pioneers that came later.

15. Fred Wilbur Powell, ed., "Introduction," *Hall J. Kelley On Oregon: A Collection of Five Of His Published Works And A Number of Hitherto Unpublished Letters* (Princeton: Princeton University Press, 1932), vii-xxi. Powell points out that Kelley was not the first or only American to promote the settlement of Oregon. Henry Brackenridge first raised the subject in 1814 in his *Views of Louisiana*, which sparked the interest of Thomas Hart Benton who, after becoming a U.S. Senator, recruited Representative John Floyd and others to lobby Congress on behalf of Oregon. However, Kelley is the only one to have actually planned a colony and recruited settlers, a few of whom eventually made it, though under Wyeth's leadership. For a complete biography of Kelley and a comprehensive examination of the part he and others played in bringing Oregon into the United States, see: Fred Wilbur Powell, *Hall Jackson Kelley, Prophet of Oregon* (Portland, Ore: The Ivy press, 1917).

16. Powell, *Kelley on Oregon*, 71-92. On his town site drawing, Kelley used "Wappattoo" for Sauvie Island and "Multnomah" for the Willamette River. In 1926 this area was named Kelley Point in his honor by the U.S. Board on Geographic Names : Lewis A. McArthur, *Oregon Geographical Names*, 4th ed. (Portland, Ore: OHS, 1974), 403.

17. Ibid., xiii-xix.

18. Robert T. Boyd, "Another Look At The 'Fever and Ague' Of Western Oregon," *Ethnohistory* 22, no. 2 (1975): 135-136.

19. Philip Henry Overmeyer, "Nathaniel Jarvis Wyeth," *Washington Historical Quarterly* 24, no. 1 (March 1933): 28-31; Young, *Journals of Wyeth*, 79.

20. Wyeth's younger cousin John was one of those who quit. He later wrote a book criticizing Wyeth's leadership style and faulting him for recruiting young men of high society who signed on for a quick profit and were not prepared for the extreme hardship and risks the trip entailed: John B. Wyeth, *Oregon: or a Short History of a Long Journey from the Atlantic Ocean to the Region of the Pacific by Land*, in *Early Western Travels*, 1748-1846 no. 21, ed. Reuben Gold Thwaites (Cleveland: Arthur H. Clark, 1905), 28-31, 65-67.

21. Overmeyer, "Wyeth," 28-31. For a detailed listing of Wyeth's men and what happened to each of them, see: Philip Henry Overmeyer, "Members of First Wyeth Expedition," *Oregon Historical Quarterly* 36, no. 1 (March 1935), 95-101. Overmeyer was working from a list published in Cambridge prior to the group's departure: "Wyeth's Expeditions," Vertical File, OHS. Pierre's Hole is a narrow valley in Idaho, just west of the Tetons in Wyoming. This rendezvous was the largest gathering of mountain men in history, so Tibbets would have met Joe Meek, Robert Newell, and others who later settled in Oregon. See: Jim Hardee, *Pierre's Hole!: The Fur Trade History of Teton Valley, Idaho* (Pinedale, Wyo.: Sublette County Historical Society, 2010).

22. Karen Bassett, Jim Renner, and Joyce White, *Oregon Historic Trails Report* (Salem, Ore: The Oregon Trail Coordinating Council, 1998), 104; Young, *Journals of Wyeth*, 154.

23. Powell, *Kelley on Oregon*, xiii. Frank Tebbetts ,who claimed a family relationship with Calvin Tibbets, said he came from Portland, Maine: Fred Lockley, *History of the Columbia River Valley from the Dalles to the Sea* (Chicago: S.J. Clarke Publishing Company, 1928), 3:434.

24. Nathaniel Wyeth had convinced his brother Jacob to join the American Society while planning his own expedition, so both are included in Wyeth's recruiting numbers, not Kelley's: Overmeyer, "Wyeth," 29. Overmeyer, "Members."

25. Powell, *Kelley on Oregon*, 308.

26. Overmeyer, "Wyeth," 30-33; Young, *Journals of Wyeth*, 56.

27. Young, *Journals of Wyeth*, 178.

28. No full length biography of Nathaniel J. Wyeth has been written. For biographical sketches of his life and expeditions, see: LeRoy R. Hafen, ed., *The Mountain Men and the Fur Trade of the Far West* (Glendale, Cal.: A. H. Clark Company, 1968), 5:381-401; Overmeyer, "Wyeth," 28-48; John A. Wyeth, M.D., "Nathaniel J. Wyeth and the

struggle for Oregon," *Harper's New Monthly Magazine* 85, no. 510 (November 1892): 835-847. For a full length but fictional account, see: Christian McCord, *Across the Shining Mountains: The Odyssey of Nathaniel Wyeth* (Ottawa, Ill.: Jameson Books, 1986).

29. Robert Carlton Clark, *History of the Willamette Valley, Oregon* (Chicago: S.J. Clarke, 1927), 228.

30. Oliver Tatum, "Matthew Deady (1824-1893)," *Oregon Encyclopedia,* http://oregonencyclopedia.org/articles/deady_matthew_1824_1893_/#.V1IPYXn2Z5x (accessed June 3, 2016); Matthew P. Deady, "Annual Address," *Transactions of the Third Annual Re-Union of the Oregon Pioneer Association* (Salem, Ore: E.M. Waite, Steam Printer and Bookbinder, 1876), 24.

31. William G. Loy et al., *Atlas of Oregon*, 2nd ed. (Eugene, Ore: University of Oregon, 2001), 14.

32. Hubert Howe Bancroft, *History of the Northwest Coast* (San Francisco: A. L. Bancroft & Company, 1884), 2:598. Bancroft personally wrote this volume according to: William Alfred Morris, "The Origin and Authorship of the Bancroft Pacific States Publications: A History of a History – I," *The Quarterly of the Oregon Historical Society* 4, no. 4 (1903): 287-364. Any citation to one of Bancroft's histories that Morris attributes to Francis Fuller Victor will show her as the author.

33. Archer Butler Hulbert, ed., *The Call of the Columbia: Iron Men and Saints Take the Oregon Trail* (Colorado Springs: Stewart Commission of Colorado College and Denver Public Library, 1934), xiii, 111.

34. Bassett et al., *Trails Report*, 99,101.

35. Powell, *Kelley on Oregon,* 99; John Ball, *Born to Wander: Autobiography of John Ball, 1794-1884,* eds. Kate Ball Powers, Flora Ball Hopkins, and Lucy Ball (Grand Rapids, Mich.: Grand Rapids Historical Commission, 1994), 61.

36. Nellie Bowden Pipes, "Extract from Exploration of the Oregon Territory, the Californias, and the Gulf of California, Undertaken During the Years 1840, 1841 and 1842 by Eugene Duflot De Mofras," *The Quarterly of the Oregon Historical Society* 26, no. 2 (June 1925): 168. Duflot de Mofras listed seven French Canadians who had begun farming before 1833, three starting in 1833, and fifteen more from 1834 to 1837.

37. John Ball and Kate N. B. Powers, "Across the Continent Seventy Years Ago," *The Quarterly of the Oregon Historical Society* 3, no. 1. (March 1902): 103-104. John Ball, *Born to Wander*, 61, 63, 83-120, 155. Jean Baptist Deportes McKay was often referred to as "Depaty" and similar nicknames—likely due to the length of his full moniker. He should

not to be confused with Thomas McKay, who was a stepson of John McLoughlin and had a farm nearby: Corning, *Dictionary of Oregon History*, 161. For comprehensive coverage of the impact of the diseases of white men on the Indians of Oregon, see: Robert T. Boyd, *The Coming of the Spirit of Pestilence: Introduced Infectious Diseases and Population Decline among Northwest Coast Indians, 1774-1874* (Seattle: University of Washington Press, 1999), 242-261.

38. Powell, *Prophet of Oregon*, 148.

39. Overmeyer, "Members," 99; "Mission Record Book," MSS 1224, OHS, 16-17. These sources give only Sargent's first initial. HBC journals give his full first name: "Abstracts of Servant's Accounts," York Factory/Northern Department: B.239/g/12 (1833), 13 (1834), and 14 (1835), Hudson's Bay Company Archives, Winnipeg, Canada (HBCA).

40. Overmeyer, "Members," 100-101. The Smiths have descendants still living in the area: "'Celiast' and 'Ilchee'," http://trailtribes.org/fortclatsop/celiast-and-ilchee.htm (accessed June 3, 2016).

41. Ball, *Born to Wander*, 39-40, 60. One way in which Ball's attitude manifests itself is his never naming Tibbets or others he did not see as his equal in society— unless they were unique, like his host McKay.

42. Shawna Lea Gandy, "Fur Trade Daughters of the Oregon Country: Students of the Sisters of Notre Dame De Namur, 1850" (master's thesis, Portland State University, 2004), 2-3. Lower case "métis" will be used throughout this book, since it takes the place of "mixed-blood" and does not refer to the Red River valley communities in Manitoba: a convention described by Gandy that seems appropriate. Terms like "half-breed" will not be used except in direct quotes.

43. "Journal of Rev. Jason Lee," *Christian Advocate and Journal* 16 (August 25, 1841). This article was missing from historical news service databases, but Corey Flick, research librarian at the Methodist Library at Drew University, was kind enough to locate it and send a digital copy by email on November 21, 2012. It is cited in: Cornelius J. Brosnan, *Jason Lee, Prophet of the New Oregon* (New York: Macmillan, 1932), 162.

44. Solomon Smith recalled his friend Tibbets living with an Indian woman during the years they were on the Willamette, but said that she did not come with him to Clatsop Plains: "Probate Journal 2," Clatsop County Probate Records, Oregon State Archives, Salem, Ore (OSA), 29. Methodist and Catholic records show no record of a formal marriage. Nor is there any record of her full first name. She was most likely Kalapuyan, since that was the tribe living in the area, and women from other tribes were brought there by their trapper husbands.

45. "Recapitulation of Book Debts," Fort Vancouver Account Books: B.223/d/66 (1834), 73 (1835), 86 and 88 (1836), HBCA.

46. Samuel Asahel Clarke, *Pioneer Days of Oregon History* (Portland, Ore.: J.K. Gill Company, 1905), 1:205. Willie McKay was a son of the Thomas McKay mentioned in note 37, thus a grandson of John McLoughlin. He became a physician and settled in Pendleton. He was a student of both John Ball and Solomon Smith at Fort Vancouver: Corning, *Dictionary of Oregon History*, 161.

47. Brosnan, *Jason Lee*, 44-46, 72. The Methodists had accompanied Nathaniel Wyeth's second expedition most of the way. Their first mission location is now a park near Wheatland: http://oregonstateparks. org/index.cfm?do=parkPage.dsp_parkPage&parkId=99. (accessed June 3, 2016).

48. Frederick V. Holman, "A Brief History of the Oregon Provisional Government and What Caused Its Formation," *The Quarterly of the Oregon Historical Society* 13, no. 2 (June 1912): 113-115. Holman published a list put together by George Himes (first secretary of the Oregon Pioneer Association and OHS) that showed the religion of each person who voted at Champoeg on May 2, 1843 on "who's for a divide." Congregationalists were most closely aligned with the Presbyterians; Methodists were a competing group. See: Congregation Library and Archives, "The Congregational Christian Tradition," http://www.congregationallibrary.org/researchers/congregational-christian-tradition (accessed January 27, 2014).

49. See note 47; Nellie B. Pipes, "Journal of John H. Frost, 1840-43 [Part 1]," *Oregon Historical Quarterly* 35, no. 1 (1934): 64. Pipes had Rev. Frost's first name wrong; it was actually Joseph: Corning, *Dictionary of Oregon History*, 94.

50. The temperance society was formed by the Methodists on February 11, 1836. Within a week eighteen men had joined, but their names were not recorded until January 2, 1837: Charles Henry Carey, "The Mission Record Book of the Methodist Episcopal Church, Willamette Station, Oregon Territory, North America, Commenced 1834," *The Quarterly of the Oregon Historical Society 23, no. 2 (1922): 242, 250;* for details on the Presbyterian version, see: *Oregon Spectator,* July 8, 1847.

51. Stephen Dow Beckham, "Oregon History: Souls to Save," *Oregon Blue Book,* http://www.bluebook.state.or.us/cultural/history/history08.htm (accessed June 3, 2016). What brought missions to Oregon was a story about Flathead and Nez Perce Indians journeying to

St. Louis in 1831 asking for the white man's religion. This was at best a misunderstanding due to lack of proper interpretation. The tribes wanted nothing to do with white religion; they had their own belief systems that worked just fine for them: Comments by Wilson Wewa, Warm Springs Washat leader, OHS Death Symposium November 7, 2013. Additionally, the tribes were so decimated by disease brought by whites that there were soon not many to convert: White, *Misfortune*, 71.

52. Powell, *Kelley on Oregon*, xiv-xvii.

53. Bassett et al., *Trails Report*, 94-113.

54. F. G. Young and Joaquin Young, "Ewing Young and His Estate: A Chapter in the Economic and Community Development of Oregon," *The Quarterly of the Oregon Historical Society* 21, no. 3 (September 1920), 230; "E. Young to Mr. Tibbets, November 3, 1837," *Willamette Cattle Company*, MSS 500, OHS; Lawrence H. Officer and Samuel H. Williamson, "Seven Ways to Compute the Relative Value of a U.S. Dollar Amount, 1774 to present," *MeasuringWorth*, http://www.measuringworth.com/uscompare/ (accessed June 3, 2016).

55. Stephen Dow Beckham, "Oregon History: Federal Interests," *Oregon Blue Book*, http://www.bluebook.state.or.us/cultural/history/history07.htm (accessed June 3, 2016). Though only in Oregon for three weeks, Slacum's report was extensive: Forsyth, "Slacum's Report," 210-213; David T. Leary, "Slacum in the Pacific, 1832-37: Backgrounds of the Oregon Report," *Oregon Historical Quarterly* 76, no. 2 (1975), 118-134.

56. Cornelius J. Brosnan, "The Oregon Memorial of 1838," *Oregon Historical Quarterly* 34, no. 1 (March 1933): 69.

57. James K. Kelly, "Annual Address," in *Transactions of the Tenth Annual Re-Union of the Oregon Pioneer Association* (Salem, Ore: E.M. Waite, Steam Printer and Bookbinder, 1883), 8-13.

58. Forsyth, "Slacum's Report," 196-197.

59. Ibid., 208-209.

60. Kenneth Munford and Charlotte L. Wirfs, "The Ewing Young Trail," (Horner Museum Tour Guide Series, 1981), available at http://www.bentoncountymuseum.org/index.php/research/sites-of-interest/horner-museum-tour-guide-series/the-ewing-young-trail (accessed June 3, 2016). Orin Kay Burrell, Professor of Finance at the University of Oregon, went so far as to say: "The cattle drives which came decades later on the Chisholm trail from Texas to Kansas must have been more

child's play by comparison:" O.K. Burrell, *Gold in the Woodpile; an Informal History of Banking in Oregon* (Eugene, Ore.: University of Oregon Books, 1967), 15.

61. Philip Leget Edwards and Douglas S. Watson, *The Diary of Philip Leget Edwards; the Great Cattle Drive from California to Oregon in 1837* (San Francisco: Grabhorn Press, 1932), available at http://www. catl.com/DiaryOfPhilipLegetEdwards (accessed June 3, 2016); William M. Colvig, "Indian Wars of Southern Oregon," *The Quarterly of the Oregon Historical Society* 4, no. 3 (September 1903): 230. The names of those wounded are not given.

62. "George Foster Emmons' diary, 1838-1842" (New Haven: Yale University Photographic Service, Yale University Library, 1978), September 29, 1841, viewed on Microfilm 182, OHS; Henry Eld, *Wilkes Expedition: diary of Passed Midshipman Henry Eld, 7 September 1841 to 29 October 1841* (New Haven: New Haven Colony Historical Society, 1947), 29; Henry Eld, "Clamet [*Klamath*] Valley" map with notes for travel on September 29, 1841 in original journal, WA MSS 161, Beinecke Rare Book and Manuscript Library, Yale University, New Haven, CT. [None of these sources have page numbers, so dates will be used, all in 1841]; Jessie Poesch, *Titian Ramsay Peale, 1799-1885, And His Journals of the Wilkes Expedition* (Philadelphia: American Philosophical Society, 1961), 192.

63. Smith and the missionaries had first built cabins a few miles south on Clatsop Plains proper (forest covers the land between), but by the time Tibbets arrived they had determined it was too remote and difficult to get supplies there. Wallace, a black deserter from the *Maryland*, also helped them with the construction: Daniel Lee and Joseph H. Frost, *Ten Years in Oregon* (New York: J. Collard, Printer, 1844), 294-296.

64. William S. Hanable, "USS Peacock wrecks at the mouth of the Columbia River, giving her name to Peacock Spit, on July 18, 1841," *HistorLink.org*, http://www.historylink.org/index.cfm?DisplayPage=output. cfm&file_id=5624; (accessed June 3, 2016).

65. "Historic Reminiscences In Clatsop Nearly Fifty Years Ago: Personal Narrative of Rev. W.W.Kone, A Man Who Saw the 'Peacock' Wrecked in July 1841," *The Weekly Astorian*, April 27, 1889, reprinted in the *Cumtux* 4 no. 3 (Summer 1994): 10-14; It was especially difficult for Emmons to watch the *Peacock* sink because he had served on it since its inaugural voyage: "Emmons' diary," July 20.

66. "Emmons' diary," July 22. In this entry Emmons notes the instructions from Wilkes, who had been there earlier to make arrangements, but had left to explore along the Washington coast while waiting for his other ships to arrive from Hawaii. Hudson had been captain of the *Peacock* when it floundered. The Expedition in total included "six sailing vessels and 346 men, including a team of nine scientists and artists" that would "cover the Pacific Ocean from top to bottom" over five years: Nathaniel Philbrick, "The Scientific Legacy of the U.S. Exploring Expedition," *The United States Exploring Expedition, 1838-1842*, http://www.sil.si.edu/digitalcollections/usexex/learn/philbrick.htm (accessed June 3, 2016)

67. In orders to Emmons dated July 31, Hudson wrote that "the man Tibbits [*Tibbets*] who you wrote for was off in the mountains with Mr. Dana – he will probably arrive on Monday next." On the bottom of the orders, Emmons makes a note, "Rec'd by Messenger sent from Ft Vancouver while between 4th and 5th Encampments," which would have been August 7, but the orders are microfilmed after his diary entry that combined July 29 and 30. Reference to Tibbets being on his way are in the orders from Lt. Hudson to Lt. Emmons dated August 2, 1841: "Emmons' diary," August 5. Emmons refers to having "sent to employ as a guide" Tibbets and Warfield as well as McKay. Others who have written about the climb of Saddle Mountain only mentioned Indians guiding Dana, and made no mention of Tibbets, likely because "Emmons' diary" has not been transcribed, much less published. One example that provides references to others is: E.W. Giesecke. "First Recorded Ascent of Saddle Mountain: List of Climbers," *Cumtux* 4 no. 3 (Summer 1994): 14-15.

68. "Emmons' diary," August 11.

69. Ibid., August 17. Others who quit were Cornelius Rodgers and men Emmons identified only as Conner and Saunders.

70. Ibid., September 7 and October 8; Eld, MSS 161, "Sasty [*Shasta*] or Cascade Mountains Continued" map with notes on travel for October 8. Neither Emmons nor Eld name Warfield's wife, but she is named in the Catholic record of their marriage and baptism of all family member on September 14, 1840: Harriet Duncan Warner and Mikell DeLores Warner, trans., *Catholic Church Records of the Pacific Northwest: St. Paul, Oregon, 1839-1898, V. 1-3* (Portland, Ore.: Binford & Mort, 1979), 16-17.

71. "Emmons' diary," September 5-7; Ibid., September 29. Emmons also named creeks after Robert Newell on August 5, and Joe Meek on August 6, while they were guiding him across the Tualatin Plains.

Emmons' description of Tibbets Creek best fits Pass Creek as it passes through Curtin. Emmons was naming the creeks after Americans because he did not like the British naming Mount Hood after one of their own. On August 6 he wrote, "I think we should be allowed the privilege of naming some of the most beautiful & prominent features of our Country after our own good and great men." Wilkes did not evidently agree with Emmons' position because when he wrote the official expedition report he did not include Emmons' naming of the creeks. Since Emmons' diary was never separately published, his names for the creeks did not take hold.

72. Richard H. Dillon, *Siskiyou Trail: The Hudson's Bay Company Route to California* (New York: McGraw-Hill, 1975), 285-286; "Emmons' diary," September 6. Emmons does not name Tibbets as Whitcomb's choice to care for his bulldog, but Dillon does. Tibbets is the mostly likely choice because Whitcomb had lived with him at the Clatsop mission earlier that summer, where he had gone for health reasons: Lee and Frost, *Ten Years*, 306; Pipes, *Frost Journal*, 167. The full group roster is at: "Emmons' diary," September 7.

73. Lee and Frost, *Ten Years*, 324. Brainard evidently did not stay long at Clatsop Plains because he helped establish the Oregon Rangers in response the to the Cockstock incident in 1844: James Henry Brown, *Brown's Political History of Oregon* (Portland, Or.: W.B. Allen, 1892), 127-130.

74. "Emmons' diary," October 29; Ibid., October 28. On October 20, Emmons wrote that Sutter "expressed himself much in want of clerks and labourers [*sic*]." Sutter was a major employer in that era of California history. See: "John Augustus Sutter," *New Perspectives on the West*, http://www.pbs.org/weta/thewest/people/s_z/sutter.htm (accessed June 3, 2016).

75. James Warfield Probate Case File No. 0610, OSA. Francis Fuller Victor suggested that Tibbets came back with Joseph Gale: Victor, *History of Oregon*, 1:249n50. But Gale did not return to Oregon until May of 1843: Clarke, *Pioneer Days of Oregon History*, 627. Published HBC records do not mention the Americans tagging along with Ermatinger's brigade either. It is only because James Warfield died on the trip home that the manner in which Tibbets returned home is known. Letters between Ermatinger and some of the other Americans refer to him. Whitcomb's bulldog is not mentioned.

76. Victor, *History of Oregon*, 1:188.

77. Robert H. Ruby and John A. Brown, *The Chinook Indians:*

Traders of the Lower Columbia River (Norman: University of Oklahoma Press, 1976), 203-212; Lee and Frost, *Ten Years*, 309-330. Just after arriving at Clatsop Plains, Frost had witnessed HBC hanging a Quinault Indian for the murder of an employee and his Clatsop helper at their Pillar Rock fishery: Ibid., 270-274.

78. Dobbs, *Men of Champoeg*, 5-6.

79. Fred Lockley, "Impressions and Observations of the Journal Man, "*Oregon Daily Journal*, May 1, 1936.

80. "Tozier From Wash. Co. Museum Files," Albert Tozier Collection, box 4, folder 1, MSS .001, Washington County Museum Research Library, Portland, Ore.

81. Ibid. Many of Tozier's letters credit his elders for instilling in him a life-long interest in Oregon history which motivated him to get to know many of the earliest settlers of Oregon, both French Canadian and American, and led to his being caretaker of Champoeg.

82. Emma Gene Miller, *Clatsop County, Oregon, a History* (Portland, Ore.: Binfords & Mort, 1958), 98-99.

83. "Probate Journal 2," 28-30.

84. Lyle Anderson, *Warrenton's History 1792-1992* (privately printed, 1992), 35.

85. "P.W. Gillette Dead," *The Sunday Oregonian*, January 22, 1905; "Pioneers of Oregon," *The Morning Oregonian*, January 18, 1896. Gillette also said it was very hard to grow wheat in the sandy soil of Clatsop Plains.

86. Provisional Government Document # 40, 1174; MSS 1226 Microfilm, OHS. Sarah Damron Owens (mother of Dr. Bethenia Owens-Adair) includes a Marlin (most likely Henry) in her list of neighbors building the mill, and she leaves out Edward Williams: Bethenia Owens-Adair, *Some of Her Life Experiences* (Portland, Ore: Mann & Beach, Printers, 1906), 152. The list of owners used here comes from the incorporation papers. Owens refers to Ohanna Creek, which was a common name at the time for the Neawanna River. It was also known as Wahoni Creek, as indicated by the name of the milling company. The mill changed hands not long after being built and was converted to a saw mill. It was a landmark for residents of Clatsop Plains well into the 20th Century. It was mostly likely located where Mill Creek enters the Neawanna just north of the bridge on Highway 101 that separates Seaside and Gearhart. For a comprehensive history of this and other mills of the area see: Liisa Penner, "The First Seaside Mills" (unpublished paper, September 8, 1993, Clatsop County Historical Society).

87. "Probate Journal 2," 28-30. Neighbors give conflicting testimony on when John was born. A female minor, but no male minor, is listed in: Julie Kidd, abstractor, *1845 Census of the Territory South of the Columbia and West of the Cascade Mountains* (Portland, Ore., Oregon Territorial Press, 1997), 10; John Tibbets is named, and his age given as four, as a member of Solomon Smith's family in: Lisa Penner and Judi Byrd, abstractors, *Clatsop County, Oregon Territory, 1850 Federal Census* (Astoria, Ore: Clatsop County Historical Society, 1986), 10. This would place John's date of birth in late 1845 or early 1846, after and before the dates that the respective censuses were taken. Rev. Frost always referred to Tibbets as a bachelor. Since he left Oregon the middle of August 1843, it is most likely that Calvin and Louisa came together between then and the first of January 1844, when new neighbors arrived. These later testified in probate court as having always known Calvin and Louisa to be together.

88. Merk, *Oregon Question,* 247. John Minto arrived in Clatsop County in 1844. He later recalled "the race prejudice against Indian and negro blood the American home builder brought with him from Missouri to Oregon 60 years ago.": October 30, 1903 Letter to F.G. Young, box 1, folder 6, MSS 752, OHS.

89. The only three residents of Astoria when Adair arrived: Lockley, *Columbia River,* 1:240.

90. E.E. Rich, ed., *The Letters of John McLoughlin from Fort Vancouver to the Governor and Committee: Third Series, 1844-46* (Toronto: Champlain Society for the Hudson's Bay Record Society, 1944), 73.

91. "Probate Journal 2," 28-30. Neighbors gave conflicting reports on Tibbets intent as far as marrying Louisa. The overall impression is that over the years his intent changed in favor of formal marriage, but that she resisted because she did not understand the custom and was confused by it; Sylvia Van Kirk, *Many Tender Ties: Women in Fur-Trade Society, 1670-1870* (Norman: University of Oklahoma Press, 1983), 50.

92. Ruby and Brown, *Chinook Indians,* 213.

93. Dorothy Baerveldt and Peggy Enlund, ed., *History of the Pioneer Presbyterian Church of Clatsop Plains,* 2nd ed. (Warrenton, Ore.: privately printed, 1981), 12; *Oregon Spectator,* July 8, 1847.

94. After Geer jumped ship he offered to pay Clatsops to kill Rev. Frost because he hampered sales. When Frost heard of this he asked Indian agent Elijah White for help. White worked with John McLoughlin, who packed Geer out with the next HBC overland express to Eastern Canada: Clarke, *Pioneer Days of Oregon History,* 411.

95. In telling the story, William Gray explained that, though he was presiding judge of Clatsop County's Court, he had assigned Tibbets to the case because Oregon's Provisional Supreme Court had appointed him prosecutor: *Oregon Spectator*, July 22 and August 5, 1847. Tibbets was first appointed as a judge by the provisional government for a one year term: Joseph Gaston, *Portland, Oregon, Its History and Builders: In Connection with the Antecedent Explorations, Discoveries, and Movements of the Pioneers That Selected the Site for the Great City of the Pacific* (Chicago: S.J. Clarke Pub. Co., 1911), 1:122. William Perry had been appointed for three years, but resigned after the first year, so the Supreme Court appointed Tibbets to serve Perry's second year: Lawrence T. Harris, *Oregon Supreme Court Record* (Portland, Ore.: Stevens-Ness Law Publishing Co., 1938), 1-2, 26. There is no record of Tibbets having any legal training, but the same was true of his fellow judges. During the provisional government period the population of Oregon was so small that people were selected for positions based on character more than training.

96. "Letter to the Probate Court of Clatsop County from the Trustees of the First Presbyterian Church of Clatsop Plains," September 3, 1850, Calvin Tibbets Probate Case File No. 235, OSA.

97. Baerveldt and Enlund, *Pioneer Presbyterian Church*, 3, 12, 22. As this history of the church points out, the original building is long gone. In the church history, and all other records available, Robert and Nancy Morrison (Tibbets' neighbors to the south) are given sole credit for contributing the full ten acres of land the church owns. This is legally correct, and proper title is not being questioned here. Provisional land claims were abolished by the law that established the Oregon Territory in 1848. Settlers had to refile after the Donation Land Claims Act passed in 1850, which Tibbets was not able to do since he had died in 1849. As soon as the Clatsop County Probate Court was appointed, church trustees asked them to clarify their situation on multiple occasions but they did not (see "Probate Journal 2"). At some point everyone likely realized that Tibbets' provisional land claim was moot, and that all the Morrisons had to do was move their claim north far enough to include all of the church property (they had given the church five acres of their claim at the same time as Tibbets), and then gift it to the church once they proved up. Robert Shortess, the guardian of Grace and John, sued the church and other property owners who, from his perspective, had jumped Tibbets' claim, saying the children should

have inherited his rights to it. Shortess won in Justice Court, but the Oregon Supreme Court overruled it in "Robert Shortess v. A.E. Wirt" which silenced other cases as well: Joseph G. Wilson, *Reports of Cases Argued and Determined in the Supreme Court of the Territory Of Oregon and of the State of Oregon* (San Francisco: Bancroft-Whitney Company, 1887), 1:90-91.

98. William G. Loy, Stuart Allan, and Clyde P. Patton, *Atlas of Oregon*, 1ˢᵗ ed. (Eugene: University of Oregon, 1976), 24. The reason they give for the depression is an oversupply of wheat. For extensive coverage on the impact of the California gold rush on Oregon, see: Victor, "Chapter II," *History of Oregon*, 2:43-65. Many of these men had just dragged their wives and children 2000 miles across the Oregon Trail. Now they left them to tend crops, care for livestock, and protect provisional land claims from being jumped by newcomers: White, *Misfortune*, 208-209. This mass exodus caused businesses, newspapers, and even the provisional government, to shut down for a time. Fortunately, most of these men returned home with enough gold to justify the sacrifices they and their families had made, and the cumulative increase in wealth gave a much needed boost to the Oregon economy: P.W. Gillette, "Forty-Eight Years Ago," *The Sunday Oregonian*, December 16, 1900.

99. Owens-Adair, *Life Experiences*, 159, 217; *Oregon Free Press*, September 30 and October 7, 1848. Some authors have said the ship was called the *Skipanon*, likely because it was built at Skipanon Landing; but all firsthand sources confirm it was called the *Pioneer*. A discussion of where it might have been built and what it might have looked like can be found in: Anderson, *Warrenton's History*, 41, 44-46. Elbridge Trask sailed to Oregon as part of Nathaniel Wyeth's second expedition and did some trapping in the Rockies before settling on Clatsop Plains. In 1852 he moved to Tillamook: Carla Albright, "Elbridge Trask," *Oregon Encyclopedia*, http://oregon-encyclopedia.org/articles/trask_elbridge_1815_1863_/ #. Vo2Z2Xn2Z5w (accessed May 31, 2016). Receipts show that Tibbets boarded with Trask (who lived at Skipanon) while building the *Pioneer*: Probate No. 235.

100. Coastwise Entries, June 16, 1849; Journal 1, 1849—1872; Entrances and Clearances, 1849-1939; Collection District of Astoria, Record Group 36; National Archives and Records Administrations—Pacific Alaska Region (Seattle).

101. Fred Lockley, "Impressions and Observations of the Journal Man," *Oregon Daily Journal*, May 1, 1936. Owens-Adair was the first

female physician in Oregon, and notable in other ways. For a comprehensive biography, see: Carol Kirkby McFarland, "Bethenia Owens-
Adair: Oregon Pioneer Physician, Feminist, and Reformer, 1840-1926"
(master's thesis, University of Oregon, 1984).

102. "Saw 'Pioneer' Launched," *The Morning Astorian*, November 2, 1916.

103. The Oregon Territory was created by Congress August 14, 1848,
and Astoria designated a Port of Entry. Governor Joseph Lane arrived
in Oregon City March 2, 1849 to begin work: Ruby and Brown, *The Chinook Indians*, 212-213.

104. See note 100.

105. "Marine Journal," *Oregon Spectator*, October 4, 1849; "Passage
from San Francisco," Probate No. 235; "Probate Journal 2," 9. Various
authors have said Tibbets died on the *Forrest, Ocean Bird,* and the
Priest but probate journal and case file information prove it was the
Anita.

106. Owens-Adair, "Life Experiences," 217.

107. Probate No. 235; Officer and Williamson, *Measuring Worth*.

108. In the same year that Tibbets estate settled (1854), Oregon paid
Joaquin Young $4994.64 after he came forward to claim the estate of
his father Ewing: Young, "Ewing Young Estate," 201.

109. Robert Shortess was appointed guardian of the children September 4, 1850, the second day of the probate court's first session, so
Louisa had died by then: "Probate Journal 2," 2. No reason is given for
Louisa's death; just a receipt for her funeral. Charges for board and
room of the children dominate the receipts: Probate No. 235.

110. Several cases are listed in "Probate Journal 2."

111. Gandy, "Fur Trade Daughters," 137-144, 217. Gandy indicated via
email on May 7, 2013 that she had mistaken the nineteenth century
French cursive writing of Tibbets as "Cibbats (Gibbars)."

112. "Probate Journal 2," 29. See note 107.

113. Grace Tibbits [*Tibbets*] (aged 15), Oregon City, Clackamas, Oregon, "1860 Unites States Federal Census." Database. *Ancestry.com*,
http://www.ancestry.com (accessed June 3, 2016)

114. Grace Tibbetts [*Tibbets*] married October 29, 1877, "Washington
Marriages, 1802-1902." Database. *Ancestry.com,* http://www.ances-
try.com (accessed June 3, 2016); Ralph Franklin and Joe Hayes, *Northwest Black Pioneers: A Centennial Tribute* (Seattle: BON Marché,
1994), 14; Descendants live in Oregon, Washington, Montana, and California: email from Roberta Kelley, received March 13, 2014.

115. Calvin Tibbets is mentioned in twenty-three issues of the *Oregon Historical Quarterly*—including the first—as well as some of the Oregon Pioneer Association *Transactions* and hundreds of other journals and books; but mostly in passing by writers focused on someone else, or an event rather than the people involved. The most extensive biographical coverage of Tibbets is in: Caroline C. Dobbs, *Men of Champoeg; a Record of the Lives of the Pioneers Who Founded the Oregon Government,* 2nd ed. (Portland, Ore.: Metropolitan Press, 1993), 35-40. Even Dobbs spends most of her time talking about those associated with Tibbets, and some of her information is incorrect.

"Emigrants to the West" by William Cary, opposite page 310 in A Popular history of the United States, Volume IV, by William Cullen Bryant and Sydney Howard Gay (1881).

Made in the USA
Charleston, SC
31 August 2016